The Longevity is Killing Us Series - Book Three

AMERICA'S PUBLIC ENEMY

#1

is

AMERICA'S PUBLIC

WANTED ALIVE

Richard W. Farwell

RUGGED MAN PUBLISHING

America's Public Enemy #1 is America's Public Wanted Alive

The Longevity is Killing Us Series – Book Three

Printed in the United States of America.

Cover design by Lyndsey Barrett, www.AreteDesignStudio.com.

ISBN-10: 0985314915
ISBN-13: 978-0-9853149-1-0

Published by Rugged Man Publishing.
www.ruggedmanpublishing.com.

Dedicated to all the world's children
whose future is being mortgaged by their parents

Table of Contentious Content

An Introduction... To Foolish or Misplaced Disregard

Twenty-six years ago, on October 19, 1987, I started a financial planning practice. The big market hit that day did not reflect our strong underlying economy. I and most of my clients enjoyed 13 years of dollar-cost-averaging success.

Late in 2000, I predicted the dot.com bubble would burst soon. Some followed my advice by reducing or eliminating holdings in the dot.com/high technology stocks all represented in the NASDAQ market index. I also recommended that holdings in the overall stock market be reduced as it would suffer along with technology holdings. Most did not. The NASDAQ is still 20% below that high of 5000 more than 12 years later. When inflation is considered, the NASDAQ would have to rise to 6800 just to break even. Our high tech leaders at present (Apple, Facebook and Google) are working hard on a new bubble. More on that later.

In 2005, I recommended that clients consider selling their real estate as did I near the high of the market. A few did, while most waited and watched the real estate market hold up for a few more years then crumble as the Great Recession of 2008 hit hard. Early is better than late in many ways.

Early in 2007, I sensed severe weakness in the developed world, namely USA, Europe and Japan. We all were developed economies with aging societies. So I wrote a booklet, "Longevity is Killing Us," which is a solution to federal budget deficits supported by more debt. The key principles of the book are living a long, full, healthy life but a short, unhealthy one...and suggesting that we citizens in a republic must recapture our supreme power by taking it back from the politicians. Consistent with my past vision, it did not and still is not selling well.

Near the end of 2007, I sold my practice; and my departing recommendation was to again cut back on a weakening real estate market, risky real estate debt securities and stock market equities because of what I learned while earning and maintaining five professional designations. Simply said, I learned that the best way to invest is to buy low and sell high. All of the mortgage-backed securities sold throughout the world were based upon one underlying asset... USA real estate, which was in bubble territory.

Did you read about the $13 billion in fines against JP Morgan in November 2013? They were accused of misleading investors including Fannie Mae and Freddie Mac regarding the mortgage-backed securities they were selling leading up to the Great Recession. While I avoided the 2008 Great Recession, most did not.

I totally disagree with the charges against JP Morgan. They were selling high. That is typical, strategic and sound. Buying high is wrong, regardless of so-called AAA ratings. It was the buyers and their advisers who caused the Great Recession, not the greedy Wall Street capitalists.

If you truly want to control greed, then fine. Support progressive tax rates while simplifying our tax system. With tax reform, the successful but greedy will not be able to work the complex system we have to their advantage. Of course, tax deductions should be allowed. The most important ones are for charity and business expansion if it results in domestic job growth.

Walmart is a great example of how a big business should be run. They buy wholesale at low prices from around the world... repackage and add a small profit margin. They then sell low so customers can buy low. Their profit comes from volume and basic consumer needs, not from greed.

In 2012, I wrote a new booklet, "You Pledge What?" It was an extreme example of how the majority of Americans have undermined all of the principles of our Pledge of Allegiance. America is a republic, one nation under God, indivisible, with liberty and justice for all. Even though the words are repeated regularly, we have given up our supreme power; we are becoming a nation under human nature, not under God, and are totally divided with liberty and justice for some, not all.

This final writing of mine will briefly explain why America is weakening, what will happen if we do not dramatically change our thoughts and ways and why I fly my flag at half mast. Surprise... that has also been ignored or just not noticed!

The Path We Are On

Imagine you are headed to Europe or Japan. You have no cash and have exceeded your credit limit. If you must stay on your present path, how long can you hold your breath until an implosion occurs?

While my record of predicting economic events over the past 26 years has been right on and mostly rejected or ignored, I cannot give up hope for tomorrow. I do not want the coming implosion. I want to be wrong this time. Unfortunately, I'm afraid I will again be right, as there is not one sign I see giving me any kind of hope for an awakening. Think about having 47 million Americans on food stamps, etc., etc.!

In the last election, the majority of Americans supported more government control, more restrictions and regulations on business, resulting in more budget deficits, more debt, more unfunded entitlement liabilities and weak economic growth all in the name of fairness (i.e., we must teach the greedy capitalists a lesson).

There is nothing wrong with using debt as a stimulus when an economy is weak. It is called Keynesian Economics and is a perfect kick start. Nevertheless, replacing capitalism with debt stimulus over a long period of time (i.e., since 2008) is a clever trap that is nothing more than a Keynesian key to catastrophe.

High and rising healthcare costs are not only overwhelming our federal budget, but elderly parents and grandparents only make it worse with their human nature-driven goal of costly and often painful longevity. Yes, "Longevity is Killing

Us," (the title of my first book in this series) and why will be clear after reading Chapter 7.

What is really happening here is not due to political campaigns, the left vs. the right or media power.

Both of our major political parties approach issues of importance or even unimportance with clever brevity. Think, if you will, abortion, amendments to our Constitution, environment, greedy capitalists, immigration, IRS scandal, Obamacare, public unions, etc. You will soon learn on the following pages why so many Americans buy brevity.

Politicians, corporate leaders, organizational executives dare not nail our shallow electorate for fear of losing votes, customers, and contributors, respectively. While some conservatives will comment about the mortgage on our children's future, they join their opposition in blaming each other... not the real culprits.

As a driver, you should know what I learned before retiring as a race car driver... how much safer it is passing on the left. Since we often approached 150 mph while passing on straight-aways, the SCCA (Sports Car Club of America) would black flag us (back to the pit for the day) if we did not follow that rule.

As a young American or parent of one, you should know what I learned before retiring as a financial adviser... how politically, economically and financially dangerous it is to allow the left to pass on debt and dependency to future generations. Pardon the driving analogy, but the accelerating left pass we are supporting can only lead to a deadly collision with America's tomorrow. Now that's the real pits!

Why Not Reverse Course?

Plenty has been written over the years about why global citizens are distracted from the truth about the future.

While none of the experts will describe so many citizens as shallow like I do, the sophistication of those brilliant minds reveals many reasons for humans to be totally distracted. Here are just a few of the subtle, undermining blinders:

Happiness

I have never read a better synopsis on happiness than the July 8, 2013 article in Time magazine about this subject... "The Happiness of Pursuit."

Here are a few quotes you may find revealing about the distracting subtleties of seeking happiness. Reading the whole article is a must for most:

"So it's possible that being distracted may also reduce our own happiness." Sylvia Morelli, Neuroscientist, Stanford University.

"Money can make you happy, but it's about how you spend it." Ryan Howell, Psychologist, San Francisco State University.

"Happiness is not a goal, it is a by-product." Eleanor Roosevelt.

"The only way to do great work is to love what you do. If you haven't found it yet, keep looking. Don't settle." Steve Jobs, Apple Inc. Co-Founder.

My take is less sophisticated. Too many people rely upon smartphones, social media, french fries, alcohol, gambling, tattoos, clothing, cars, etc. These are things, not experiences... just other forms of self-fulfilling failure and sadness. Buying happiness is temporary and sets one up for accepting shallow input in the form of sophisticated subtlety.

Education

Of all the subtle forces driving the public to take stands for or against multiple issues, none are as uniquely subtle as education.

In a perfect world, all educators would offer strengths and weaknesses for each subject giving students the opportunity to decide for themselves the position to take on issues involving politics, the environment, our economy, etc.

Of course, most educators are public employees, so they will naturally lean toward more government... especially in the case of economics where a balanced discussion about budget deficits and unfunded public pension liabilities could be embarrassing.

Since there has been so much written criticizing our system of learning, I do not place any resultant blame on teachers for their imbalance just as I do not blame politicians for our divided country.

Teachers should warn all students, especially those graduating from college, of the risk of finding a good job with benefits in a weak economy dominated by a powerful government that relies more upon debt than real economic growth.

That said, it does not matter to me if they do or do not offer balance to their students as long as students are taught more critical thinking skills. The thought, whether taught in school, at home or wherever, is self-analysis for each subject. All humans should develop the ability to look at any situation, analyze and then logically infer what the outcome will be and who might lose.

When a student is exposed to a subject and then comes away with a strong or leaning position for or against either side, he or she should then have the ability to look at the opposing side and analyze the situation from other points of view. In doing so, students can minimize or even eliminate subtle mind manipulation. Think french fries or fruit? Smartphones or smiles?

In fact, the concept applies well beyond education. All humans, especially in this high tech, accessible world of information, can apply the strategy to all positions thrown at them by government, business, media and even friends and relatives. In doing so, we cannot only avoid mental manipulations mandated by many, but we can also allow supply and demand (a form of freedom) to minimize the losers eliminating costly and controlling rules, regulations and enforcement. Think fracking or fuel efficiency? Drones or privacy? Red wine or tequila shots?

Inflation

As subtle as the subjects of happiness and education are in driving the thoughts of most humans in the developed world, inflation should not be in that same class.

Sorry, but it is alive and well disguised. When citizens in the developed world of late have voted to increase the cost of goods and services they need and want to consume, the results can be nasty domestically but great for low-cost exporters like China.

As American majorities have supported more government and less economic growth through their shallowness, we now have a political standstill/standoff in Washington, DC, with liberals wanting more restrictions on business and conservatives wanting less.

Those decisions, created in the voting booth, have resulted in our central banker, the Federal Reserve Bank, expanding our money supply as a temporary stimulus to the economy. Their goal is to keep interest rates low and inflation near 2%. Unfortunately, with weak economic growth forcing businesses to outsource, use more technology and hire part-time workers with few benefits, wages cannot keep up. It's ironic that so many middle class Americans helped create such a political stalemate and then suffer the most.

Government Control

As subtle as seeking happiness, obtaining an education and inflation are, they are overwhelmingly dominated by the gradual and growing power of discreet government control.

Although a conservative, I agree with democrats that we need to reduce the size and power of big banks. What about big agriculture, big medicine and worst of all... big government? More restricting regulations simply mean more government power. The cost of federal regulations is now half of the federal budget.

In the last 20 years, we have approximately 82,000 new federal regulations, and the Dodd-Frank regulations following the 2008 Great Recession are only 40% completed! Regardless of these and the hundreds of thousands of state and local regulations across our great nation, they are small and at the edge of insignificance compared to the serious issues of an aging society.

The Affordable Care Act (Obamacare) seeks to control 17% of our economy! If Google and their new project of extending life expectancy succeeds, healthcare costs will only rise further along with more government control.

We need financial reform and fewer regulations so our small businesses have a chance.

Our financial markets are now a bigger part of our economy while the real economy has slowed. Financial markets are too short term vs. a real economy which should be long term.

America is overruled and over-regulated. If you don't believe me, just watch a football game! Who do you think is controlling the game? Is it the coaches, the quarterback, the offense, the defense or just perhaps the officials?

Yes, capitalism in the form of big business should be restrained through reforms, not more control... so we can get back to former greatness.

Anti-business policies have limited economic growth and may never be enough to cover our rising government costs. The wealthy get most of that growth. Unemployment numbers are misleading, as so many have given up looking for a job. While middle class wages are not keeping up with inflation and rising costs of real life, the majority of Americans keep voting for more of the same! Wow!

Does what's happening in Detroit and Chicago raise any eyebrows? Seems not...

I understand that, as a nobody, few will listen to me. What about Ted Cruz, the junior Senator from Texas? He is a somebody and believes that only Americans, not politicians, can solve our healthcare issues. He also believes, as do I, that our Social Security system is a Ponzi scheme and should be privatized as well as many other government agencies being eliminated. Good luck, Senator.

The bottom line is we need economic growth that is stronger than inflation, since the latter is a hidden tax on growth. It will not happen, though, while the majority of Americans are cleverly and subtly brain gamed. Throw in the gaming of happiness, education and government control plus many more mind manipulations and we may never get a needed course reversal. It seems most people don't want to give up the luxuries of life... even if borrowed, not earned.

My Awakening

After the last national election in November 2012, the statistics that followed overwhelmed me! The majority of women, our young and Hispanics voted for more government control, more deficits, debt and dependence.

How could a woman, especially if a mother, support more government, which mortgages the future of her children by placing the issue of abortion ahead of motherhood? Do not get me wrong, ladies. I am not trying to throw a Bible your way. The truth is, if I were in the womb and could see what I see coming, I would definitely accept and support abort.

How could our young voters support more government and less economic growth and jobs, which undermines their own future? I love to exercise, kids. That said, there is no way you can build your shoulders wide and strong enough to handle the burden you are supporting.

The statistic that really blew me away was that our Hispanic voters overwhelmingly supported more government. Some of my very best friends are Hispanic. I have always been impressed by their powerful work ethic, strong family support and love of God. How could they support anti-growth policies, which undermine job opportunity? So much for work ethic! How could they support more deficits and debt which undermines their children's future? So much for strong family support! Also, why would they allow human nature to drive their decision by placing immigration issues ahead of heartfelt decisions? So much for love of God!

These issues regarding voters drove me to the first draft of this final writing of mine. As I pondered the direction a majority of Americans were supporting, I kept asking why?

I have always understood that mankind's emotional thoughts and actions based upon human nature are natural resulting in winners and losers. Those thoughts and actions starting in the Garden of Eden, or as humans developed, have been offset by heartfelt thoughts and actions seeking no losers.

The world has grown and developed because of that balance even though many still suffer today. In fact, while world economic growth has lifted millions out of poverty for centuries, many are now falling back into desperation as capitalism is being undermined.

It was early in 2013 when I started this research, but I landed in a holding pattern and came to a stop as I could not sort out why the path the developed world was on and even picking up speed. My first title for this book was "Financial Incestuousness." While that may describe what is happening, I needed to understand why it was happening. For three months, while my human transmission was stuck in neutral, my motorized brain was revving at maximum RPMs. I became so emotionally stressed by my lack of understanding that I pushed my exercise routine, my drinking and gambling as forms of distractions. Yes, I need distraction, too, if for reasons different than most.

The magical moment for me as to why human nature, with all its distractions, was defeating heartfeltness then occurred. The event was an annual community fund raising event for women's health... fabulous food, drinks, displays, a silent auction and a great stage show. Before the main event, a leader of the women's movement gave a great presentation then sat down in the front row. Next was a fashion parade by women of all ages escorted on stage by male doctors in medical uniform.

At one point, I looked across the stage where the leader was seated. She and her friend were both on their not-so-smartphones occasionally glancing up. It was at that moment when it dawned on me why distractions are overwhelming developed world societies.

You can see it for yourself. Just walk down a busy sidewalk, watch some drivers as they weave, notice many at school, in bars and restaurants. They are overwhelmed by the power of technology and social media.

Yes, we have always had exercise, sports, drugs, alcohol, gambling and in recent times radio, television and the media, etc. as distractions. What has changed, though, is a power attack on human emotions through brief, sophisticated mind games, a so-called daily messaging war of email blasts, tweets, videos, cable news sound bites and weakening but still active news in print. This daily war is also carried out by many parents, teachers, friends, businesses, bosses, politicians, doctors, charitable organizations, etc., seeking their own subtle control knowingly or not. Even my pastor has said that most humans do not understand human nature.

Want an analogy to help you understand what is happening? Here it is:

Clever, mind-manipulation chemicals are blended and injected into human nature thoughts and actions, a shallow area just below the surface of the human brain. Many humans, without considering a much deeper injection into their heartfelt thoughts seeking no losers, want only to win and gush their quick support or rejection of the input... then immediately return to their hi-tech distractions.

Call it what you may. I call it human fracking. Some believe that earthly fracking is damaging to our soil. Maybe so. Human fracking, though, is worse! It's damaging to our soul.

Like any war, the best strategy for winning is at least a two-pronged approach:

1. Distract (with "stupid-phones," iPads plus those distractions we've always had)
2. Attack (using human nature resulting in winners and losers)

The primary reason the attack (#2) is working so well is because so many of the attackers know that the victims will immediately return to their distractions (#1).

Here are some simple examples about what is winning:

- Acquiring before admiring
- Debt before delayed gratification
- Fun before fulfillment
- Getting before giving
- Moments before meaning
- Pleasure before priority
- Pressure before peace of mind

- Spending before saving

The result is that humans find little time or motivation to seek who the losers may be from their actions, which simply has left heartfelt in the dust. Another of my examples of many left behind in the dust is our costly and sometimes inefficient military. As the leader of the so-called free world, we surely need a strong military. That said, it is well beyond the limits of this writing.

What is within this final challenge of mine is the truth that strong economic growth is needed for many reasons, including helping those veterans who have served and are suffering from their sacrifice for our freedom.

When the majority of American voters allow human nature plus distractions to encourage support for economic weakness and more government control over our lives, especially those who have served, we are in effect taking the free out of the word "free"dom. That's "dom"!

You don't agree? Well, perhaps this quote from someone much more intelligent than I may help regarding the high-tech appeal to our human nature and distractions: "I fear the day that technology will surpass our human interaction. The world will have a generation of idiots."... Albert Einstein

While my awakening has occurred, a global awakening must occur sooner or never. Relying upon our government representatives to fix things is not going to happen anytime soon. The stalemate in Washington, DC, will continue until a financial, economic or social crisis brings the country to a halt. When that happens, the world will demand higher interest rates on our bonds forcing us to borrow more just to cover interest payments.

Due to the stalemate in our capitol, our central banker (the Federal Reserve Bank) is also borrowing to stimulate consumption by keeping interest rates low. That also cannot last as a substitute for capitalism. Central bankers in Europe and Japan are doing the same with little success. Our Fed has been doing it since 2008 with limited success.

A perfect example of how the power of clever mind games will continue to undermine America's future is our stock market. Wall Street used to be a great indicator of our economic progress. Consumption needs were met with business expansion and more hiring. Life was good... until our aging society combined with advances in our sophisticated medical world drove up healthcare costs to double the per capita costs throughout the developed world.

Combine those rising costs with a number of environmental issues and the result was a multitude of new government regulations restricting economic growth.

Then, along came the Great Recession of 2008. The real cause of that global economic collapse was not those greedy capitalists who packaged mortgage backed securities and sold them worldwide.

Ever heard the term "caveat emptor?" Buyer beware! I and others in the financial world warned that those securities should not be purchased as the underlying asset was American real estate in bubble territory. While I went to school a lot of years to learn to buy low/sell high, that simple truth was ignored by buyers throughout the developed world.

The result was substantial and costly investment losses, bailouts and more anti-growth regulations still being developed five years later!

Selling high is not greedy, just clever with the odds of prices dropping significantly. It is buying high that is greedy, expecting high prices to continue. Think today's lofty stock and government bond prices!

Okay, so take the stock market and the clever mind games being played on Americans. The attacks upon corporate America include a range of issues. Some of the most popular are environmental destruction, greedy capitalists, crony capitalism, etc. Attacks upon too much government control are also occurring. Attacks from both sides of our political aisle are financed by big money and are totally dividing our country. Think Koch Konservatives vs. Soros Sliberals... just more clever words describing two sources of wealthy contributors to each of our major political parties.

Successful business owners have one primary goal... make profits! Today, due to so many business restrictions supported by the majority of Americans, large companies outsource many jobs overseas where labor costs are lower. Some even borrow at cheap interest rates to buy back their stocks driving up stock prices. Domestic companies are emphasizing part-time work to avoid rising government restrictions. All businesses will continue to use technology and other cost-cutting strategies to seek profits until Americans awaken to the truth.

Here is the truth: America, just like all developed and

developing countries, needs more capitalism at home, more jobs at home, more tax revenues at home...

NOT

More anti-growth policies, more budget deficits, more debt, more dependency upon government. If you are too high-tech and don't relate to excessive government control, think government remote control. It's happening, too!

Chapter 7 will explain how we can fix our problems, make the greedy pay more and also build a social safety net for Americans who really deserve it.

Remember... businesses make profits, or they are out of business. Governments make profits (budget surpluses) or they borrow and mortgage the future. If more Americans continue to support the latter, they are making the same mistake the world made leading up to the Great Recession. The awakening that must occur is for Americans to simply look to the so-called asset underlying the packaged anti-business product being sold to them... overwhelming debt in bubble territory.

Liberal politicians are using the ultimate American "litmus" test. They want to convert our population base through debt to blue... while pouring acid on the red.

Regarding the 2014 elections, if there is an American awakening and the citizens decide to support pro-business, pro-economic growth, pro-jobs and less government control over our lives, I expect the Tea Party will dissolve and blend. They are truly grassroots and the opposite of a pyramid scheme.

Do not assume from what I have said so far that I support unrestrained capitalism – I do not! Capitalism is incentives to take risks resulting in success or failure. If we do support real capitalism along with tax reform, then big profits equal big tax revenue and big domestic employment.

On the other hand, if the majority of our voters continue to support more government dependency, I plan to cancel my American citizenship and relocate to Sweden. Of course, my wife of 40+ years will have a choice... and I will surely return regularly to visit our two children, nine grandchildren and one great one. Maybe a Hawaiian cruise and Christmas for sure. No way will I return on the 4th of July since American independence is waning! To paraphrase the wedding vow, until debt do we part! If the majority of Americans continue to support more debt, I'm out of here... it's not the country I love. Why Sweden, you ask? You may just love the answer in Chapter 7.

Obviously, the attempt to teach the greedy capitalists a fairness lesson has backfired on the middle class, as the wealth gap has widened. Has anyone noticed? Want to try a better approach... or just double down come the next election?

God's Wrath Invited

With no signs of detours or road closures ahead, either mentally or economically, the mortgage on our children's future will continue until an implosion occurs.

Think not about a single car crash analogy. We need a peaceful awakening before a huge disaster hits us all. If you believe in God... any God or higher power... then you must acknowledge that He loves all of His children, even if we do not. Oh, and regarding "a higher power," as religious as I may be, I truly believe that heartfeltness really does transcend religious thought. Non-believers are just as capable of such decisions and many do so regularly. In fact, many so-called believers will often criticize and judge, instead of compliment and forgive.

As mentioned in the introduction, I did propose a solution in early 2007 to control our debilitating healthcare costs... "Longevity is Killing Us." While it has gone nowhere because of human nature, I will briefly review it in the final chapter.

Assuming nothing peaceful does occur, I have no clue what form the implosion will take. Perhaps it will be financial, social, economic or even a major war. What I do know is that any kind of major global crisis will pale in comparison to His wrath (think disease, famine, earthquake and other major natural disasters). Or don't think, keep distracted and hit the gas pedal harder on the debt path to disaster.

Who Will Rise From the Ashes?

Believers of all faiths would surely hope and pray that the disaster I predict would lead to a global religious power. I would favor that result as well. It's not going to happen. Most religions worldwide are weakening as thought processes advance. There is no better example than the one I gave earlier in Chapter 2 regarding healthcare at end of life. While true believers accept their God's invitation to a heavenly afterlife, most so-called believers reject the call in favor of costly longevity, placing human nature ahead of their God and their children. I know it is happening, since I personally experience so-called believers practicing criticism and judgment while many atheists will compliment and forgive!

"Pour out your wrath on the nations that do not acknowledge you, on the peoples who do not call on your name." Jeremiah's prayer, Jeremiah 10:25. If there is any truth to that biblical verse, then America will not be relieved of His wrath.

A serious competitor for global dominance is China. They are currently second in economic power behind the United States. They are perfecting state controlled capitalism, are appeasing their anxious society and are avoiding the mistakes Russia made decades ago seeking world power. Also, they are actually using some of their profits to purchase assets in America and Europe.

While living in a world dominated by communism is scary, I do not believe that it will happen. China relies upon their cheap exports, which will weaken as the global economy implodes or God's wrath hits.

Without an awakening and following a global meltdown, there is only one supreme power that is capable of rising from our ashes to dominate the world.

Believe it or not, there are plenty of articles and books describing an organization that has developed and evolved behind closed doors for up to 100 years. Membership includes elite wealthy, powerful political and corporate leaders from around the world. It is their strategies that have created the potential for overwhelming global power. Here are just a few of them:

- Skillfully manipulate our emotions
- Fund both sides of conflicts and wars, then emphasize permanent peacekeeping forces to protect us all
- Attempt to control the leaders of major countries
- Here in America, FEMA (Federal Emergency Management Administration) has the power, under a national emergency, to control the country

The organization is seeking a one-world government and is called the New World Order. Some even believe it will be global corporatocracy or some blend of the two. Regardless, the bottom line will be global dominance as their strategies accumulate control and dominance through so-called help to protect mankind from our debilitating debt. We must avoid and restrict both overwhelming control by big government and big business. Research it if you dare.

Such a power will remain dormant and subtle if true economic growth, freedom and opportunity dominate dependence upon big government and big capitalism. As the so-called leader of the free world, we had better start thinking for ourselves and stop transferring our power one manipulated thought after another.

A Broad Awakening, Please

It's been said many times before and it has worked... "Time heals all wounds." Well, not this time!

Americans may choose the monumental risk of ignoring massive and rising debt, unfunded entitlement liabilities and even the precursors of city bankruptcies happening today. Since each may not hit hard for awhile, too many believe we can just keep it up and trust our leaders to make the right decisions.

Incremental changes over time leading to economic stability and strong growth through changes in government, political parties and business will not work. We do not have time for the process to heal us. It is a big mistake to take such a walk.

A recent study by leading economists concluded that our economy is still growing slowly five years after the Great Recession of 2008 because the wealth gap between the wealthy and the middle class is widening. While it's true that two-thirds of our economy is consumer spending and a weak job market does not help consumption by our non-wealthy citizens, I disagree with such a conclusion.

The widening wealth gap is just another symptom of the real cause of our weakness now being propped up by both government debt and central bank debt.

As I have emphasized on previous pages, the real problem is that more and more Americans are allowing human nature to dominate heartfelt thoughts and actions because of technological advances in sophisticated mind games and distractions.

Leading the list of Google searches worldwide in 2013 were deaths of famous men, the Boston Marathon bombing, seeking a smarter smartphone and singers. If such search requests do not represent the world's collective mindset, what does? Just more examples of why distractions keep creating more losers than winners.

The first sooner step is the power of the vote. No, I'm not talking about the ballot booth. I'm referring to a decision now with a medical directive or at your doctor's office to reject the costly end-of-life medical decisions that are undermining our federal budget.

Consider these facts:

- Global population graying reported in www.globalagewatch.com projects that by 2050, world population over age 60 will outnumber those under the age of 15!
- America has more uninsured than other developed economies due to good health and higher health costs.
- In America, healthcare costs in the last year of life dominate lifetime healthcare costs.
- Advances in medical technology not only extend longevity but costs as well. Our healthcare costs are double the per capita costs throughout the developed world, which hurts when we are in a competitive global economy.
- Google, Inc. now has a new project seeking to extend longevity even more.

- Medicare is going broke! No profit there.

Most importantly, there is no way we can rely upon our politicians to bring healthcare costs down. They are driven by lobby power and their placing of re-election ahead of the country's future.

Do not assume that I oppose our Affordable Care Act (Obamacare). It will be fixed or fail. Regardless of its future, it will not provide the social safety net we really do need. There is no good reason for our young, healthy citizens being forced to buy health insurance to provide a safety net for seniors and the needy. Economic success will bring the revenue needed to help them.

Also, I have no problem with Obamacare leading to some form of single payer healthcare in America. I don't need long hospital stays and the medical profession keeping their Hippocratic promises to extend my life, meaning I don't need expensive drugs or health insurance or even a government "death panel" deciding what should happen to me at life's end! I believe in a long, full healthy life and a short unhealthy one. Multiply me times all Americans or the world's citizens and we bless our children with a future worth living for! Think hospice, not hospitals. Think comfort and care, not cure.

It is estimated that our unfunded entitlement liability is between $90-100 trillion and growing. It is made up primarily by public pensions, Medicare and Medicaid. While healthcare obligations in an aging society dominate pension costs, the latter is also a big issue ignored by big government supporters.

Decades ago the majority of private industry basically exited the pension world (defined benefit plans) in favor of 401(k)s (defined contribution plans) where the employer and employees often share the investment with real money.

While pension reform is also desperately needed in America, public unions are the biggest opposition regardless of its mortgage on our children's future. Public unions would rather push the unfunded liability into the future just like most Americans want to push real debt into the future. Private industry can't do that... they either make a profit or go out of business!

What most American voters are clueless or just ignorant about is that those unions use some of the dues public employees are required to pay to fund political contributions, fighting pension reform and supporting more government. If I am not mistaken, some of America's income tax paid is not only paying public salaries and mandatory dues, but also political contributions we may oppose. Sure, public employees may "opt out" if they do not agree with such politics. How many really do that? How fair is that?

Oh, you don't agree? Fine... just keep breathing, spending and expecting your elected officials to keep their jobs by trying to over-regulate then borrow against our children's tomorrow to cover budget shortfalls, etc., etc., etc. Some politically correct call it inter-generational theft. Sorry, but it's too late to be that polite. I call it financial incestuousness, and it can only be corrected when we citizens take back our supreme power as a republic as described in the dictionary. Our children just may love us more if we do so.

You have very simple choices if you really love your children, grandchildren and everyone else's in the world. Just exercise, eat well and make decisions from the heart. Think compliments and forgiveness, not criticism, control and judgment.

Regarding compliments, I cannot restrain myself when it comes to the country of Sweden. Okay, perhaps I was a little bit facetious regarding my citizenship in Chapter 4, My Awakening. Nevertheless, here is why I have even considered my great crepe escape...

Sweden had a serious economic collapse in the early 1990s as did many global economies. They were hit especially hard due to their large welfare state in a weak economy.

Their economic reforms since then included:

- High individual tax rates
- Low corporate tax rates
- Tax and pension reform
- Sizable reduction in government spending
- Pro-economic growth reforms

And the results include:

- Export-oriented diverse and competitive economy
- Maintains a generous welfare state
- 90% of all resources and companies are privately owned

- High standard of living
- Low inflation
- Strong economic growth
- Government budget surpluses
- 70% of labor force unionized but independent of government and political parties
- Public debt has been cut in half in the last decade
- 60% of Swedes confirm their tax return by phone

Yes, Sweden is small compared to the USA with only 9.5 million residents. Yes, we are much more complex with more global responsibility. That said, we sure could learn from them about sustainability and generosity through economic freedom.

Any subsequent changes will surely take some time, but thinking clearly will help. And, speaking of help, just imagine how pure thoughts about tomorrow will help our children, our country and our global neighbors while keeping supreme power wannabes in check.

The next time you give your Pledge of Allegiance, focus on the word "republic." In a republic, the supreme power rests with the electorate... that's us! Let's keep it... by acting sooner and rejecting mind manipulations that have led to our financial folly. We are better than that, and our kids deserve more than that... not more *of* that!

Sooner or Never

Here is my recap on what must happen sooner vs. never:

1. Promote and support more economic growth through real capitalism along with a simplified tax system. Tax revenues will increase as will our domestic job market.
2. Emphasize a long, full healthy life and a short, unhealthy one. In other words, make more heartfelt decisions and stop allowing the clever mind games along with sophisticated distractions to drive your human nature, which often results in losers. This will reduce government healthcare costs and, combined with #1, will move budget deficits to surplus and stop our debilitating debt increases.
3. Support pension reform by emphasizing real cash contributions into real stock, bond and other investments. This strategy will stop the unfunded public pension promises that can never be fully paid for without more debt, which we cannot afford.
4. Emphasize to your children and grandchildren that educators and others may not have the time and/or desire to describe the winners and losers as a result of their input. Our youth must seek the truth and read between the lines regarding all important subjects while moving distractions to a secondary role in life. So must the rest of us as well.
5. Our high-tech world should develop a balanced truth test service so all could research the good and bad of all human input.

While more could be said here, these are the key issues in reversing the financial incestuousness that is happening here and abroad. If our direction is not reversed soon, then we are playing into the hands of a one-world government where all freedom is lost. Before that occurs, the world will be facing numerous economic crises, social upheavals and even the wrath of God. What each of these or a combination thereof will do is just accelerate the dominance of a global empire.

Yes, America's public enemy #1 is America's public. We must awaken and take back our Republic sooner – or never.

About the Author

75 and married – 41 years

2 children, 9 grandchildren, 1 great one

Retired:

- US Navy
- CEO, NBC Employees Federal Credit Union
- President, Farwell Financial
- CFP, Certified Financial Planner
- CFS, Certified Fund Specialist
- CRC, Certified Retirement Counselor
- Stock Broker
- Insurance Agent
- Race Car Driver

Publications:

- How Flat is Your Retirement?
- Longevity is Killing Us
- You Pledge What?

Vision:

- Physically – weakening with age
- Financially – as acute as ever

Hearing:

- Physically – weakening with age
- Financially – no one's listening

Made in the USA
Monee, IL
04 November 2026

67381287R00026